1991

P9-AQV-417

THE FACTS ABOUT

THE PHYSICALLY DISABLED

BY
Connie Baron

EDITED BY
Maythee Kantar

CRESTWOOD HOUSE
New York

CIP

LIBRARY OF CONGRESS CATALOGING IN PUBLICATION DATA

Baron, Connie.
The physically disabled

(Facts about)
Includes index.
SUMMARY: Discusses various diseases and conditions that can cause physical disabilities,
including arthritis, multiple sclerosis, muscular dystrophy, cerebral palsy, and visual and hearing
impairments.
1. Physically handicapped—Juvenile literature. [1. Physically handicapped.   2. Diseases.] I.
Kantar, Maythee. II. Title. III. Series.
HV3011.B36   1988   362.4—dc19   88-21554
ISBN 0-89686-417-0

| International Standard Book Number: 0-89686-417-0 | Library of Congress Catalog card Number: 88-21554 |

PHOTO CREDITS

Cover: Globe Photos, Inc.: Don L. Black
Journalism Services/SIU: 23, 24, 25, 26
DRK Photo: (Robert Holland) 19
Globe Photos, Inc.: (Don L. Black) 4, 7; (W. R. Stanton) 31
Tom Stack & Associates: (Brian Parker) 9, 14; (Don & Pat Valenti) 42-43
Ned Skubic: 33
Taurus Photos: (Norman R. Thompson) 10; (L.L.T. Rhodes) 17, 21, 28, 36; (Glyn Cloyd) 35, 40

Macmillan Publishing Company
866 Third Avenue
New York, NY 10022
Collier Macmillan Canada, Inc.

CRESTWOOD HOUSE

Printed in the United States of America
First Edition
10   9   8   7   6   5   4   3   2

TABLE OF CONTENTS

Although a physically disabled person may look and act differently, they still need to be liked and accepted by others.

NOT ALWAYS UNDERSTOOD

Pretend you and your best friend are going shopping. Just before you reach the door, a van pulls up to the curb. A man and woman unfold a platform behind the sliding door. They carefully push a couple of kids in wheelchairs out onto a platform, which lowers them to the ground. Then they lift a girl with crutches down to the sidewalk. A brace on her leg reflects the morning sun. You notice her eyes too. They look different than yours—filmy and white. As you weave your way around all their equipment, you see a boy on crutches putting his arm around a kid in a wheelchair. "Which department should we check out first, Johnny?"

Johnny looks at his friend. He spits a little when he answers back. "How about tennis shoes and bathing suits?"

You and your friend look at each other, surprised. Why would a guy in a wheelchair need tennis shoes or swimming trunks?

Physically disabled people need the same things we all need: clothes, homes, food, fun, and love. Being physically disabled does not mean a person stops living or feeling.

Having a physical disability means a part or parts of your body do not work right. Some people are more disabled than others. They may look and act different than you and your friend. But they still want to be liked and accepted by others—just as you do.

Sometimes it is hard to know what to do when you see a disabled person. Do you look the person in the eye and smile? Do you ignore the person? Should you hold the door open, or ask if you can help?

There are no easy answers. In this book you will read about some disabling diseases and conditions. Understanding these disabilities might help you find your own answers to these questions.

IGNORANCE, RESEARCH, KNOWLEDGE

Years ago, people with disabilities were thought to be slow and stupid. They were locked up in madhouses and treated like animals. Sometimes children born with disabilities or deformities were kept hidden in closets. Many were sent to orphanages. Certain people even believed the disabled were possessed by demons.

In those days, people did not understand disabilities and they had no way of treating them. For most people, daily life—cooking, cleaning, making clothes, farming—took almost the whole day. There was little time left to care for and teach the disabled.

Today, the physically disabled receive the treatment and attention they need to succeed.

People like Helen Keller, Ann Sullivan, and other pioneers in education for the deaf and blind showed us that the disabled deserve the same education and opportunities as everyone else. Since then our understanding of disease has grown, and so has our acceptance of the disabled.

Doctors don't know the causes of every disease, but they have learned the causes for some. Understanding a disease's cause often leads to its cure or prevention (stopping something before it begins).

Polio, for example, is nearly unheard of now. But as late as the 1950s it was a severe disease. Many people died. Some people with polio had to wear braces or use wheelchairs. Some patients had to live in breathing machines called iron lungs. But in 1954, Dr. Jonas Salk and Dr. Albert Sabin discovered *vaccines* for polio. A vaccine does not cure a disease. A vaccine works with the body to prevent disease. Today almost all babies get a polio vaccine, so very few people get the disease anymore.

Another disease that once killed many people was *tuberculosis*, or TB. Those who survived TB were confined to months of bed rest. But now, because of new health standards and a vaccine, the number of people with this disease is quite small.

Discovery of new medicines also helped get rid of some disabling diseases. Penicillin was discovered in 1928 by Sir Alexander Fleming. If you've ever had strep throat, you've probably had a penicillin-type medicine. Penicillin helps cure infections that in the past caused deafness, blindness, and other permanent disabilities.

Doctors are always looking for new vaccines and medicines. Someday, maybe the diseases and disabilities in this book will no longer exist.

ARTHRITIS

Hold your arm straight out. Now bend your wrist. You are able to bend your wrist because you have a joint between your arm and hand. There is a joint at every moveable part of your body—feet, toes, fingers, jaw, and back. A joint is a place where two bones meet. The end of each bone is covered with *cartilage.* Cartilage is a tough, white substance. It is flexible and somewhat slippery. Cartilage helps the bones move over each other smoothly and painlessly.

People with arthritis have difficulty moving because their joints don't work right. With one kind of arthritis, *osteoarthritis,* the joints don't work right because of old age.

A healthy person's joints are smooth. A person with osteoarthritis has joints full of jagged edges and pits. The surface of the joint becomes bumpy as the cartilage wears away. And as the cartilage wears

Having a physical disability means a part or parts of a person's body do not work right.

Wheelchairs could not stop these people from traveling to the French Alps.

away, rough edges meet rough edges. Moving starts to feel like the joints are squeaky, rusty door hinges.

Osteoarthritis normally starts in the joints that do the most work—hips, knees, and the lower spine. These joints carry most of our weight. A person with osteoarthritis may have a hard time doing things like cleaning or walking. Rest, medication, diet, and a special exercise program can help ease the pain.

More people have osteoarthritis than any other kind of arthritis. The wearing down of cartilage happens slowly. Some people with osteoarthritis feel no pain and don't even know they have it. Others have a lot of pain and must work hard to move.

Arthritis is normally thought of as a disease that involves swelling. But osteoarthritis causes very little swelling. In other kinds of arthritis though, swelling causes many problems.

RHEUMATOID ARTHRITIS

Rheumatoid arthritis is the most serious kind of arthritis because it deforms and cripples. Doctors have not figured out why people get rheumatoid arthritis, but they think it may be caused by one type of *virus* (a virus is a very small particle of matter that causes disease).

One of the first signs of rheumatoid arthritis is joint pain. The joint feels hard to move. Then the same thing happens in another joint. The second joint is normally on the opposite side of the body. This is why doctors say rheumatoid arthritis moves symmetrically. It does the same thing on each side of the body.

After the joint has been stiff for some time, it becomes swollen or inflamed. Doctors say this kind of swelling looks cigar- or sausage-shaped because it grows so fat and round. When the joint is swollen, it becomes even more difficult to move. The muscles around the joint become tense and pull closer together. Then the bones that meet at the joint *fuse,* or grow, together. After bones fuse, the joint no longer moves. People with rheumatoid arthritis become disabled because they can no longer use those parts of their body.

Before 1949, there was no treatment for rheumatoid arthritis. But in that year, a doctor discovered *cortisone.* Cortisone is a hormone, or chemical, our bodies make. Some hormones help us grow, give us strength, and aid in healing. The hormone cortisone helps reduce swelling. When a person takes cortisone to get rid of swelling, rheumatoid arthritis is slowed down.

But cortisone does not cure rheumatoid arthritis. Its effects last only a short time, so it must be given to a patient over and over again. It is not always a medicine doctors can use. Cortisone has *side-effects.* A side-effect is something extra that happens when you take a medicine. Usually, we don't want side-effects to happen. For example, someone who takes an aspirin to get rid of a headache may end up with a stomach ache. Stomach aches can be side-effects of aspirin. With stronger medications, side-effects are more serious. Because of cortisone's side-effects — weight gain, mood swings, soreness — doctors need to look for other medications for rheumatoid arthritis.

With most types of arthritis the best treatment is a combination of rest and *physiotherapy.* Physiotherapy is gentle exercise guided by a specially trained person. This exercise keeps muscles in shape. Physiotherapy also helps keep the muscles from tightening and slows down the crippling effect of rheumatoid arthritis.

MULTIPLE SCLEROSIS

You can blink your eyes when you want to because your brain and nerves work together. The brain sends messages through the nerves. The nerves carry messages just as a garden hose carries water. If the hose gets stepped on, the water cannot get through.

Something like the stepped-on garden hose happens to people who have *multiple sclerosis,* or MS. Their nerves do not get stepped on, but they do get a little squashed. The casing around the nerves becomes damaged and grows hard. This hardness is actually scar tissue. "Sclerosis" means scar. "Multiple" means many. The person who has multiple sclerosis has many scars on his or her nerves. The scars stop messages from getting through, just like stepping on the hose stops the water from getting through. When the muscles stop getting messages, they start to weaken and die.

The first *symptoms*, or detectable signs, of MS show up in a person between the ages of 20 and 40. The person might feel numbness as when an arm or leg is "asleep," or tingling as after an arm or leg "wakes up." People with MS may feel tired, as though they never get enough sleep, even through they rest all the time. Some people with MS feel as though they have

weights on their arms and legs.

People with MS are not always affected in the same way. Some people look and seem fine. They may have no other symptoms than fatigue and weakness. Some people can't see clearly, while others are completely paralyzed. Only one out of three people with MS is unable to walk, however. The person who can't walk uses a wheelchair, brace, walker, or crutches. These aids help the person stay independent.

The symptoms of MS can come and go. A person may not even think he or she is sick. This makes it difficult for a doctor to decide if a patient has MS or not.

A person with MS may have "attacks," "episodes," or *exacerbations.* These words all mean the disease is getting worse. More messages from the brain are not getting through, and more muscles lose control.

Sometimes the symptoms go away. This is called *remission.* When people go into remission they may not have any symptoms for weeks or years. Then just as quickly as the symptoms went away, they can return.

Even though 250,000 people in the United States have MS, nobody knows its cause. There is no test for the disease, either. It is one of those diseases that just happens. Doctors do know that more women than men get the disease. And more white people get MS than black people. Doctors also know that people who live in places where the weather is mild have a

Some people with MS need to use braces and crutches.

better chance of getting sick with MS. MS is not *contagious.* Children cannot inherit it from their parents. People hardly ever die from it.

MS can be frightening because doctors have no way to treat it and there is no cure. Researchers are looking for a cure and some day they hope the disease will be wiped out. Organizations like the National Multiple Sclerosis Society help MS victims and their families live active lives. The society offers education, helps pay medical bills, and loans out special equipment.

MUSCULAR DYSTROPHY

Have you ever seen the annual MD telethon on television, or an MD poster child? The telethon and the poster child raise money to find a cure for MD.

MD stands for *muscular dystrophy.* Muscular dystrophy is a progressive disease, which means its symptoms get worse as time goes on. Unlike MS, MD can be passed from a mother or father to a baby before it is born. MD is a fairly rare disease—only 30 out of 100,000 children are born with it.

MD attacks muscles, making them weak. Eventually they become so weak they cannot work at all, and they waste away. Almost everyone with MD becomes disabled. They are unable to move without the aid of braces, a walker, or a wheelchair.

MD attacks muscles and makes them weak and useless.

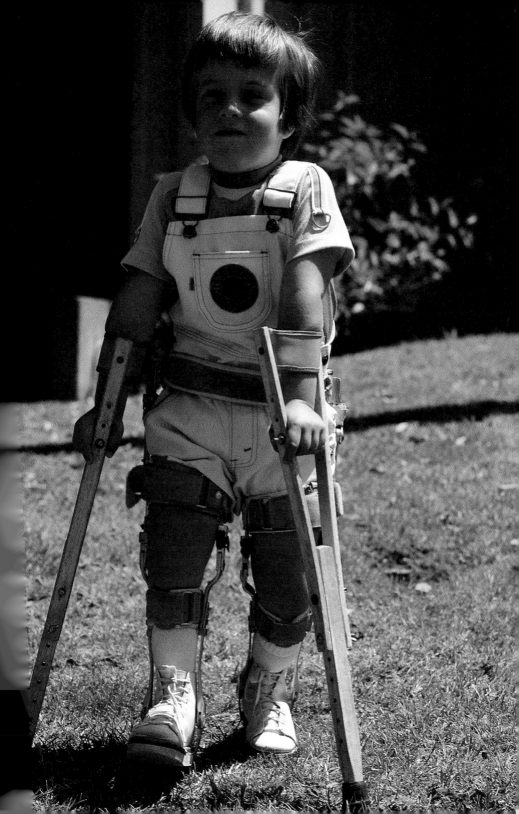

There are different types of MD. *Duchenne* is the most common form. It affects only boys. A boy with Duchenne MD will show signs of the disease before his third birthday. The first symptom is leg weakness. The weakness spreads, and the muscles are able to do less and less. A boy with Duchenne MD will probably need a wheelchair before he is 30 years old.

Doctors don't know why people get MD, although they have two ideas that seem to make sense. One is that blood flows through muscles differently in a person with MD than it does in a healthy person. The other is that muscles affected by MD are put together in an unusual way. This makes the muscles unable to do their work.

There is no cure yet for MD. But doctors can help the MD patient with surgery or physiotherapy. These treatments only make the patient's life more comfortable, however. They can not stop the muscles from decaying.

CEREBRAL PALSY

Cerebral palsy is the most common disabler of children. In the United States, almost 500,000 people have been affected by it.

Cerebral palsy is a condition, not a disease. The difference between a disease and a condition is that

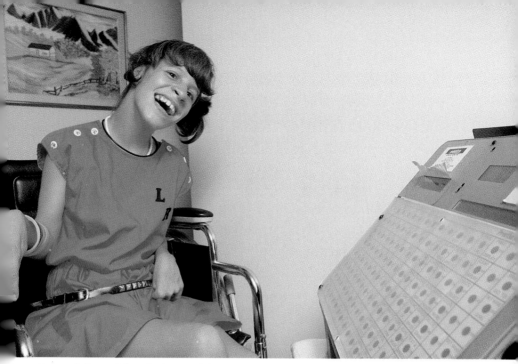

A special machine helps a girl with cerebral palsy speak to people.

a disease is a sickness. Cerebral palsy is not a sickness. Cerebral palsy happens when the brain becomes damaged.

Some people with cerebral palsy are mentally retarded. But brain damage does not have to hurt a person's learning ability. Many people affected by cerebral palsy are smart. But the brain damage stops some messages from getting to the muscles. Because no message from the brain is sent, muscles cannot move.

The brain damage can be limited (meaning small) or extensive (meaning very large and harmful). The effect of the disability depends on the amount of brain damage. A person's arm or leg may twitch. Another may not have control of his mouth and lips, so he may drool sometimes. Some people affected by cerebral palsy have only a slight limp, while others must use a wheelchair to get around.

The brain damage that causes cerebral palsy can happen before, during or shortly after birth. A mother may have had an accident while she was pregnant, or she may have gotten sick. This could have damaged the baby's brain. Sometimes during birth a baby gets into a funny position that hurts his brain. And sometimes babies fall, injuring their heads. This, too, might cause brain damage.

The treatment for cerebral palsy depends on the disability. If a person cannot straighten her legs, she might need physiotherapy and braces. Someone else might need medication or an operation. Some people whose balance has been affected by cerebral palsy wear helmets to protect their heads in case they fall.

PARALYSIS

When you get in a car, do you buckle your seat belt? Before you dive into a lake, do you know how deep the water is? Do you dive only in the deep end of a pool? If you answered "no" to any of these questions you are taking a chance of becoming paralyzed.

Diving accidents and automobile collisions cause most cases of paralysis in the United States.

Paralyzed means unable to move. Fingers, toes, arms, and legs can be paralyzed. Since it is possible for so many parts of the body to be paralyzed, doctors have come up with names for paralysis of different parts of the body. They call paralysis from the waist down *paraplegia. Quadraplegia* is the inability to move arms, legs, and all the parts in between.

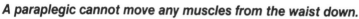

A paraplegic cannot move any muscles from the waist down.

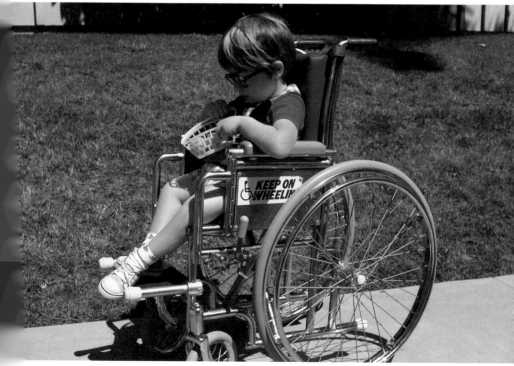

REHABILITATION

Most paraplegics, quadraplegics, and other paralyzed people want to live the same kind of life you and I do. But they need to learn new ways to do old things. They need to be *rehabilitated.* For example, if you could not stand and had to use a wheelchair to get around, how would you get the breakfast cereal from the cupboard? Could you get a drink of water from the sink? Or get up and down stairs? You would need to change your way of doing things. You would also have to change the setup of your home so you could move around easily. You might put in ramps, lower your kitchen counter, change the shape of your bathtub, or lower your bed. If you did these things, you would need less help from other people.

After rehabilitation many paralyzed people go to work, play sports, draw, paint, knit, write, and manage a house. Some paralyzed people even drive. Rehabilitation can be hard and takes a long time. But the freedom it gives makes it worthwhile.

In school and at work, new machines help paralyzed people. One computer helps a person write. It picks up light signals from a head piece the user wears. The user moves his or her head to shine the light on a letter. The computer shows the letter on the screen. By putting letters together the user can write a business letter, term paper, or memo. By pushing a

During rehabilitation, patients relearn skills like walking, eating, and writing.

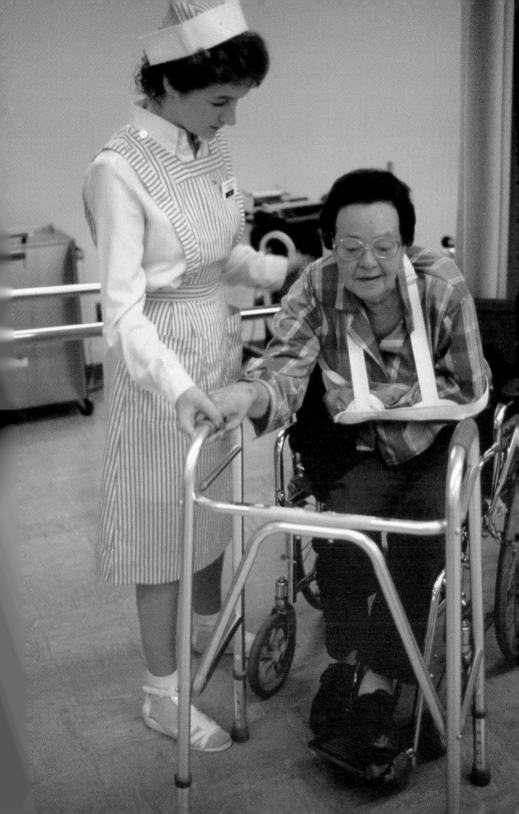

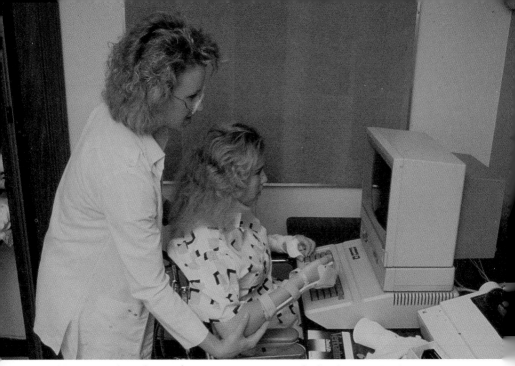

Many paralyzed people use computers to help them write letters.

button, the user tells the computer to print it on paper.

Other machines help paralyzed people talk on the phone, answer the door, and get up and down stairs. Researchers are even working with trained monkeys to help paralyzed persons. These special monkeys act as help-mates. They can pick things up, turn on the TV, hold up the phone, and do other chores!

PEOPLE WITH MISSING LIMBS

Some people are missing an arm or leg because of a *birth defect.* A birth defect means a part of the body did not develop normally before the baby was born. Other people are missing limbs because of amputation or surgical removal.

It is scary to think that someone would have to have an arm, leg, hand, or foot cut off. But amputation is done when all other ways to fix a serious problem have been used. Sometimes if the diseased body part is left on, infection can lead to other parts becoming infected.

Without certain body parts a person may not be able to walk or move correctly. That's why people missing a limb wear a *prosthesis,* or an artificial limb. With a prosthesis, a person with an amputation or birth defect can have some use of the limb.

A prosthesis is a false body part. It looks very much

A "prosthesis" is a false body part made to look like the real body part.

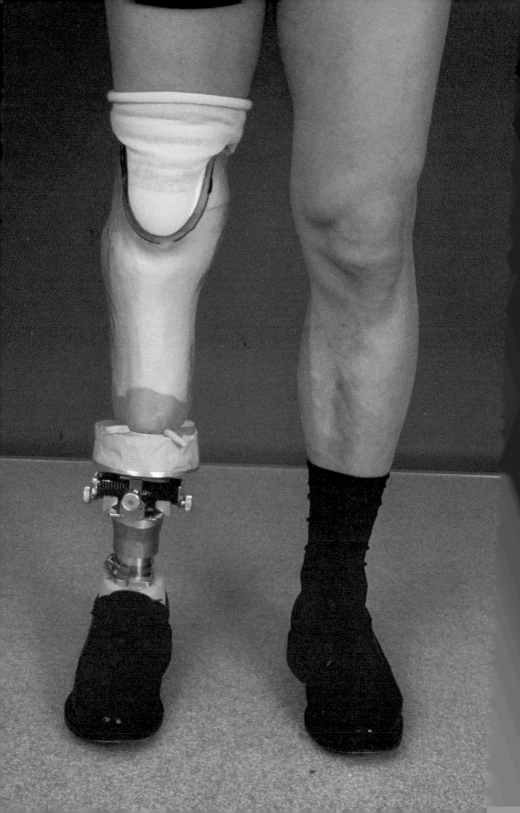

like the real thing. A prosthesis has limitations, however. Prostheses cannot bend. If a person has a leg prosthesis, he or she cannot bend at the knee. If a person has an arm and hand prosthesis, he or she cannot move the fingers or wrist. The prostheses that people use now can help do small tasks, but doctors are working on newer models that will work just like real limbs.

You might remember a TV show called *The Bionic Man* or one called *The Bionic Woman.* The bionic man and woman had computerized prostheses. Their prostheses were science fiction, but some day they may be a reality. Right now researchers are working on computerized limbs. These prostheses will feel more like regular skin and will work more like our own arms and legs.

THE VISUALLY IMPAIRED

Have you ever been asked to read an eye chart? If you have, you have had your eyes tested. During an eye test, the doctor or nurse checks to see how well you see at different distances. The doctor might say you have perfect vision. That means you can see things far away or close up with no problem. Or the doctor might say you need glasses.

But glasses cannot help everyone see well. Even

Some people need a leg prosthesis so they can walk without using crutches.

with glasses, the legally blind or visually-impaired person might only see from 20 feet what a person with perfect vision can see 200 feet away. Or a visually-impaired person might see only part of what a person with perfect vision can see. What the visually-impaired person sees may be dark or cloudy.

There are 120,000 to 200,000 visually-impaired persons in the United States. Only 20% are blind. The other 80% of vision-impaired people have some sight, but cannot drive or do other things that need good vision.

About half the blindness in adults in this country is due to *glaucoma*. Glaucoma causes pressure in the eyeball. In some people the pressure from glaucoma can be painful. But usually the pressure builds up slowly, and people may not realize their vision is being threatened.

Doctors can help people with glaucoma keep some of their vision through the use of medicines. However, doctors can only treat the eye and try to save as much vision as possible. Once glaucoma has damaged the eye it can never be repaired. It is important for people to have their eyes checked regularly for glaucoma.

Cataracts are another reason some people's vision is impaired. Cataracts are most common in older people, but younger people can have them, too. Cataracts are spots that form on the *lens* of the eye. These spots make it difficult for light to get into the eye. Since light is necessary for vision, cataracts stop

Some park paths are specially designed for visually-impaired people.

the normal sight process.

A person with cataracts cannot see the center of an image. If you had cataracts and looked at a dog, you might see the dog's outline and shape but not its face or features. Unlike people with glaucoma, most people with cataracts can have their vision restored through surgery.

LEARNING, WRITING, AND GETTING AROUND

The visually-impaired have to use more effort to do some things you and I do easily. It can be difficult for them to write and very difficult for them to read. Because body language makes up so much of what we say, the visually-impaired may be left out of many conversations.

For example, imagine you and a friend are talking about the fish you caught last weekend. You hold up your hands, about a foot apart, and say, "It was this big!" A visually-impaired person will not know how big the fish was. He or she cannot see your hands. When you are with a visually-impaired person, it is important to say in words what you might normally say with your hands and facial expressions.

The visually-impaired have a number of special ways to communicate. One of the oldest is a system

Visually-impaired people read Braille by feeling the raised dots with their fingers.

of reading and writing called Braille.

Braille is a system of raised dots. A person who reads Braille feels the dots with a finger. Each set of dots stands for a certain letter. There are also dots for punctuation and capitalization. Books, magazines, watches, and sheet music all come in Braille.

Today, talking computers help the visually-impaired learn math and send and receive messages. You may have already seen and heard a talking computer at the grocery store. Many stores use cash registers that "tell" you how much each item costs. The talking computer many visually-impaired people use works almost the same as the supermarket's. But instead of reading grocery prices, it picks up words from a person's voice and prints them.

Another new computer helps the blind read. It helps people read almost the way Braille does. But what the reader feels are not dots. This new computer allows the blind to read by making little movements that indicate letters. The movements are in the shape of letters and numbers. This new computer is important because it helps people read things that are not available in Braille.

"Talking books" provide education and entertainment for the visually-impaired. Sighted people read current and classic books on radio stations and the visually-impaired can listen at home. There are also phonograph records or cassette tapes of books for the visually-impaired.

The visually-impaired work hard to develop their other senses such as taste, hearing, touch, and smell. These other senses help guide them and give them clues as to where they are. The visually-impaired "memorize" places they go often. They learn to always put things back where they came from, and where doors, windows, closets, and drawers are. This memorization helps them be independent.

Visually-impaired people may use a white cane or a laser cane to get around. Only visually-impaired people are allowed to use white canes. They tap the cane in a certain pattern. The sound they hear lets

A disabled person is no different than anyone else—they like to do the same things others like to do.

them know where they are, whether to step down, and how near they are to a wall or a door.

For the last few years some people have been using a laser cane instead of a white cane. A laser cane guides the blind by using thin, powerful beams of light coming out of the tip of the cane.

Some visually-impaired people use guide dogs. Guide dogs are specially-trained animals that let visually-impaired people know many things, such as when to stop at a curb. Since a guide dog cannot tell when a signal light is red or green, the user listens to the traffic and tells the dog when it is safe to go. But, if a car is coming, the dog is taught to disobey the command. The dogs also let their masters know when something is in their paths.

A guide dog is working when it is with its master.

It is important not to pet or distract it. Even though the dogs are well-trained, these distractions could cause a problem for the dog and its master.

THE HEARING IMPAIRED

If you think hearing impaired means deaf, you are only partly right. Many hearing-impaired persons can hear some sounds. Some people miss only very high or low sounds. People who have damaged their hearing because of long exposure to loud noise, for example, may hear all sounds as muffled or muddy.

Our ears work almost the way a drum does. A drum works because a hand or stick hits it and makes it vibrate. The vibrations make sound. We have a drum in the ear, too. It is "hit" by sound waves. The movement of the ear drum causes small bones to move. The part of the ear called the *cochlea* changes the movements into signals our brains understand.

Infections, birth defects, and disease can cause hearing loss. An ear infection is serious and should be looked at by a doctor. Ear infections are especially dangerous in children. They can go undetected a long time and can make hearing difficult. Then the child may find it more difficult to learn to speak and spell.

You may have seen other children put things like beans or small objects in their ears. Beans, pencils, and other things that don't belong in the ear can cause infection and hearing loss.

Infections are not the only reason for hearing loss. *Otosclerosis* is a disease that may start early in life. It is most common in girls and seems to begin between the ages of 15 and 20. Otosclerosis does not cause hearing loss in everyone it affects. The person who experiences hearing loss from this disease, though, does so gradually. He or she may not notice any hearing change for years. The treatment for otosclerosis may be surgery or a special hearing aid.

A disability might hinder people from walking straight, but they still have the same feelings as anyone else.

Some hearing aids are worn inside the ear.

HELP FOR THE
HEARING IMPAIRED

You may have noticed when you talk to older people you sometimes need to talk louder than normal. This is because old age often causes hearing loss. Sometimes you don't have to talk louder with a hearing-impaired person because he or she reads lips or wears a *hearing aid.* A hearing aid is a small plastic machine that makes sounds louder.

Other devices, such as a TDD, help the hearing impaired use the telephone. This machine prints out whatever the person on the other end of the line says.

The hearing impaired have a way to hear the television, too. It is called closed captioning. Many shows are closed-captioned. This means that whatever is being said on the TV is also being written on the screen. More and more television programs are closed-captioned.

Some hearing-impaired persons own hearing dogs. Hearing ear dogs are very much like seeing eye dogs. They let their owners know about important sounds like the door bell, a timer, or a fire alarm.

TEACHING THE HEARING IMPAIRED TO SPEAK

A deaf person may speak differently than you or I, but they are not less smart. Children with hearing problems cannot hear the difference between sounds, so learning to speak is more difficult for them.

Most of us learn to speak by imitating what we hear. A hearing-impaired person imitates a sound or a word by how it looks and feels. Try this experiment. Look in the mirror, and say the sound "b." Notice how your lips move. Now say the sound "p." Was there a difference in the way your lips moved?

A deaf person learning to talk needs to learn the difference between those lip movements without ever hearing how different they sound. To learn this difference, a student could put her hand in front of her mouth. This will help her feel the amount of air that comes out with each sound. Knowing how much air comes out helps a student learn how to form that sound.

A hearing-impaired or deaf person may also lip read. This means he watches the way a person talks. From this and from understanding the way sounds are formed, the hearing-impaired person understands what is being said.

Many hearing-impaired people use *sign language* to talk to one another. Sign language uses arm, hand, finger, and facial movements to indicate letters, words, and expressions. In the U.S., hearing-impaired persons learn Amerslan, or American Sign Language. Many people with normal hearing learn sign language, too, so they can communicate more readily with their friends who are hearing impaired.

Hearing-impaired people use arm, hand, and finger movements to communicate.

Having a physical disability does not mean a person isn't smart.

ATTITUDES ABOUT THE DISABLED

Have you ever been with a group of people dressed in jeans and T-shirts while you were wearing a suit and tie or fancy dress? Because of the way you looked on the outside, you might have felt different than other people. You probably felt funny and out of place. You really weren't any different, though — you were still you.

Because it is so easy for us to only see the way people are on the outside, people with disabilities sometimes feel out of place. They might use a wheelchair or walk with the help of a brace or a cane. People might stare at them, tease, or make fun of them because they look different or move awkwardly.

But the disabled are no different than anyone else. They need friends, love, and fun to learn and enjoy life. They feel pain, sadness, boredom, and anger, too.

To help the disabled feel welcome and accepted, we have modified public places for them. There are special parking spots left open close to entrances of public buildings. We put in elevators and ramps for wheelchair access. We have closed-captioned TV. And there are laws that say no one can exclude the disabled.

We have to remember that being different is not "bad" and that physical disabilities do not mean a person is not smart. In fact, the United States once had a president who needed a wheelchair. Franklin Delano Roosevelt ran the country even though he was physically disabled by polio. Roosevelt is not the only physically disabled person to achieve great things despite a disability. The physically disabled work in many fields, from acting and writing to mathematics and physics.

Many physically disabled people enjoy sports—and can play them well.

Stephen Hawkins has a disability that now confines him to a wheelchair. At 46, Stephen must be fed by a nurse. He uses a computerized voice synthesizer to speak.

Stephen Hawkins is also one of the world's most respected physicists. He is a professor at Cambridge University in England. Hawkin's specialty has been researching black holes and writing new theories about the origins of the universe. He is considered by many scientists to be the most brilliant man in physics since Albert Einstein.

Hawkins continues to conduct lectures, write books, and work on his theories even though he cannot speak or move his body. He is also the father of three children.

A disability might hinder a person from walking straight, listening to a song, or lifting a heavy box. But the disabled have feelings like you do.

The next time you see a disabled person at a mall, the movies, the grocery store, or a park, treat them as you would anyone else. If it looks like they are having a problem, ask if you can help—we all need a little help sometimes.

FOR MORE INFORMATION

For more information about the physically disabled, write to:

National Multiple Sclerosis Society
205 East 42nd Street
New York, NY 10017

Muscular Dystrophy Association of America, Inc.
810 Seventh Avenue
New York, NY 10019

United Cerebral Palsy Association
1520 Louisiana Avenue
New Orleans, LA 70115

The Arthritis Foundation
3400 Peachtree Road
Atlanta, GA 30326

National Society to Prevent Blindness
79 Madison Avenue
New York, NY 10016

American Hearing Society
919 Eighteenth Street, N.W.
Washington, D.C. 20007

GLOSSARY/INDEX

BIRTH DEFECT 24, 25, 34—*A part of the body that has not developed correctly before a baby is born.*

CARTILAGE 9—*Soft, slippery material that covers the ends of bones.*

CATARACT 29, 30—*A spot on the eye's lens.*

CEREBRAL PALSY 18, 19, 20—*A condition caused by brain damage.*

COCHLEA 34—*A spiral section of the inner ear. It aids in balance.*

CONTAGIOUS 16—*A disease that can spread from one person to another.*

CORTISONE 12—*A hormone that reduces swelling.*

DUCHENNE 18—*A type of multiple sclerosis that shows its first symptoms before a person is three years old. It is most common in boys.*

EXACERBATION 15—*A period of time when the symptoms of multiple sclerosis or other disease get worse.*

GLAUCOMA 29, 30—*A disease of the eye where swelling in the eyeball causes vision loss.*

HEARING AID 35, 37—*A small device put in or behind the ear to make sounds louder.*

LENS 29—*The part of the eye that throws light onto the back of the eye to make a picture.*

MULTIPLE SCLEROSIS 13, 15, 16—*(MS) A disease that causes scaring of the nerves, making*

46

GLOSSARY/INDEX

movement difficult.

MUSCULAR DYSTROPHY 16, 18—*(MD) A disease that is present from birth. This disease affects the muscles, making them waste away.*

OSTEOARTHRITIS 9, 10, 11—*A form of arthritis. Cartilage wears away and makes movement difficult and painful.*

OTOSCLEROSIS 35—*A disease of the ear in which the bones in the ear break down and wear away causing hearing loss.*

PARAPLEGIC 21, 22—*A person who is unable to move his or her waist, hips, and legs.*

PHYSIOTHERAPY 12, 18, 20—*Gentle exercise used to strengthen diseased muscles.*

PROSTHESIS 25, 27—*An artificial body part.*

QUADRAPLEGIC 21, 22—*A person who is unable to move any part of his or her body from the neck down.*

REHABILITATION 22—*A time when disabled persons learn new ways to do regular things such as drive, talk, and write.*

REMISSION 15—*A time when the symptoms of a disease disappear.*

RHEUMATOID ARTHRITIS 11, 12, 13—*A type of arthritis. In this disease, swelling and fusing of cartilage cause a deformity and an inability to move.*

GLOSSARY/INDEX

SIDE-EFFECT 13—*Something that happens as a result of something we do. With medicines, side-effects are usually unwanted.*

SIGN LANGUAGE 38—*A language hearing-impaired persons use to talk to one another. The language uses hand, arm, finger, and facial movement to indicate words and expressions.*

SYMPTOMS 13, 15, 18—*Signs that a disease is present.*

VACCINE 8—*A medicine that works with the body to prevent disease.*

VIRUS 11—*A small particle of matter that causes disease.*